Mindful Mentions
Poems of Caring, Strength
And Courage

By
William Armstrong

De Corde Verba
Common Sense Haiku in 5-7-5 Beats

By
William Armstrong

Seeming to fall flat
Flat is the best to stand on
To gain our balance

We grow much larger
At the base of the mountain
Whose summit is love

Learning from error
We must make our own mistakes
Help when you need to

Our fat from the fire
Burning in embarrassment
Help us understand

What is the reason?
Why does everything go flat?
Help us see the seem

Rescue animals
Give them a house, safe and sound
Life is quid pro quo

Frail and fragile things
Like porcelain and crystal
Vulnerable beings

♦

I'm hurt and get slammed
Pounded by pain and panic
All nature feels it

Nature by degrees
Growth covers all, slow and steady
Frail, old as when young

Book learn all you can
Smart is not the same as wise
Learn wisdom from life

Eyes open, mouth shut
Sounds abrupt and commanding
Helps us absorb life

What is our purpose?
Is there a reason we're here?
Don't think it, live it

If you must despair
Then the greatness of humankind
Should be your reason

Deluded thinking
Like a stagnant river flow
Is clouded by silt

Are objects all one?
Or, are they separate pieces?
How do you see them?

Envy shapes itself
Cheering others' misery
The shape of sadness

To stand tall when low
Valor is courage moving
Brave action moving

Raise your standard high
Your flag should be your heart-sign
Emblazoned by love

It's a simple task
To fight the good fight, is all
Call it our mission

It's variation
Our differences make us great
Love the dissimilar

Seek diversity
You'll find that fusion is slow
We should not be pure

See us as all one
Love our disparate cultures
Global family

Do not seek beyond
Keep grounded in now
Let the after be

Ask the great questions
Use them to know yourself well
Don't fear the answers

Vacation to learn
Not only to shop and drink
View the wider world

Talking is easy
Knowing is more difficult
The sign of wisdom

Teach them common-sense
Our kids have a right to know
Teach by example

How do we do it?
Live according to nature?
To ours, or the worlds?

Be like a runner
Start at the start, end when done
The race is finite

Teach more Earth-science
Show children how it started
Helps them keep it well

To know ourselves
To know what we do and why
A reason we're here

We feed on ourselves
We are sustained by our pride
Instead of our hearts

I should obey you
You do not obey nature
How can you lead me?

Nature teaches us
We should learn her example
Still our quick anger

We know our details
Money, hobbies, attractions
We don't know our mind

How long do we have?
Gaining but never seeing
How long does it last?

Alpha, omega
This life is a finite stretch
Correct the middle

We must have the best
The best food for our bodies
What about our minds?

Our flesh is a house
Be sure to furnish it with
The best furniture

Fundamental truths
Humanity and justice
Do not know borders

Peace calls it murder
But, because of a border,
War calls us hero

Do you want comfort?
Stop pursuing happiness
You'll find enjoyment

Temporary smile
Happiness is transient
Seek comfort instead

The search can frustrate
Losing it can leave anger
Let happiness go

Settle for comfort
A relaxed and easy life
Excitement will fade

You will search for fun
If you must, then do it well
Be well and stay safe

How to look forward
You have to forgive yourself
Each of us will err

Should you forgive me?
I have harmed you, so, myself
Forgive only you

Forgiveness is right
There is someone to forgive
That 'someone' is you

Someone hurt you bad
Give the gift of forgiveness
Then, go on your way

Pursue your success
But, don't hope others will fail
Defeat, don't destroy

Success is desired
There's nothing wrong with winning
We try harder then

Sometimes we increase
We add to our life and self
When we should decrease

Lose what you don't need
Leave the unnecessary
What's unessential?

Treat real friends as gems
They are rare and enrich us
Their value is love

We don't fall in love
Someone lifts us to its heights
And lets us live there

Sharing problems helps
I've never known anyone
Without a lifefull

Where does peace reside?
Must we live in a vacuum?
Only within us

Dreaming is success
Not having dreams to pursue
Is a life stagnant

Our circumstances
They do not decide for us
How happy we are

Don't scream at the dark
Do not stumble in blindness
Let hope be your light

Be just like a child
When they are just starting out
They love everyone

What is true evil?
When we can't focus on love
Then does evil win

To those in our lives
Not all deserve our respect
At least be polite

Love what you don't get
Sometimes, not getting your wish
Means we learn something

Treat love as a car
Check the oil and fuel gauges
Then step on the gas

Choose a goal in life
Then raise the roof of your dreams
As high as you can

Who chooses your mood?
Is it your circumstances?
You alone must choose

Throw away your plans
And get ready to live life
That's the way it goes

Let peace and calm win
In this battle we call 'Life"
Serene victory

To help your brain work
Don't live for adrenaline
Relax and slow down

Excitement is fine
Its pursuit will never end
If that's all there is

Remember this, then
To avoid criticism
Do nothing at all

Some say talk is cheap
It's the cheapest gift there is
Pay the price instead

Give all that you can
Keep in step with changing life
You'll get what you want

Know what a smile is?
The best plastic surgery
You'll never pay for

If you're impatient
In any great endeavor
See it fade away

Revel in your growth
But, don't expect others to
Their eyes may be closed

Plan to be content
Write it on your calendar
Then, make it happen

Try and force your way
You trample the porcelain
Gentle is the key

Love your excuses
With them, you cannot accomplish
They keep your days free

All that's possible
Will someday be accomplished
Are you the one who…

Turn your eyes inward
You are the greatest teacher
Of your life lessons

If you are content
Suddenly, everything fits
Into your life plan

Ask 'How?' don't ask 'Why?'
When it comes to reaching out
And helping others

Life is worth living
How do I know this is true?
I make it a fact

Your soul is your food
Learn to dine as a gourmet
Love as the main dish

Safety is our search
We look for a protector
You are your own knight

Share some of your soul
Help us see our human selves
Be more than a beast

Use your confidence
But, make sure it's not ego
There's a difference

Sometimes, messy's good
It shows us we can relax
Less to worry on

Peace is not the end
It is a constant process
An ongoing goal

We look to nature
Even those in the city
To remind us all

A heavy burden
I don't look to lighten it
Just for stronger arms

Treat all people with
Justice and benevolence
If you seek to lead

World peace starts at home
We must love our own world first
Comfort, peace and strength

The effort is all
Winning comes with effort first
Work is your first goal

Truth about yourself
Know your faults and fails
Then tell us of ours

You're lucky in love?
Then, fall in love everyday
With the same person

◆

How do you know it?
How do you know it's for real?
It's new, everyday

So, it is failing
You sure your love is fading
Love or excitement?

Love of another
This should be a gift for us
Don't make it a need

Don't write down your goals
You'll need a big eraser
Make them part of you

The answer's simple
Like the search of the cosmos
It is what it is

Loves lives equally
Begin to love prejudice
And love disappears

Yesterday's stumble
Confessed in love and action
Shows wisdom today

Silence in its turn
And speaking when it's timed right
Is wisdom possessed

A daily fresh start
Awakening to new dawns
Life's recurring gifts

See the wrath you feel
Take some deep, refreshing breaths
Then course your action

Opportunity
Turned golden in ill fortune
Shows true astuteness

Fluid be your mind
Let your goals be loosely held
You'll stunt frustration

To fail is a step
Towards finding the right path
Where we find success

To see one's life scoffed
Yet to remain calm and kind
Shows where wisdom lives

Mistake sloth for love
Ignore action to find ease
You'll see life crumble

Know more your own faults
And point them out to yourself
But not in others

Maturity makes
Wisdom, love, care and concern
One's philosophy

To be full certain
Of any of life's actions
Is true court true doubt

Stumbling can help us
It wakes us when we sleep walk
And helps to guide us

Doing is progress
To know when to act or not
Stems from true wisdom

Happy is fleeting
Like all feelings, it flies fast
Be content instead

Hurricane feelings
When past, can leave us empty
And make us addicts

If you want too much
You will progress more than if
You possess too much

A dream. Life's painting
Brush stroke by brush stroke
Forms a masterpiece

What we leave our kids
Is either the quest for wealth
Or the search for wisdom

Don't paint for the blind
Nor compose for the deaf
Wisdom for the wise

To glut is discord
Neither too many nor few
Sing moderation

Don't deny too much
To starve is to watch life fly
We are consumers

Be part of the view
Life is a kaleidoscope
Move with the turning

A smirk can hide pain
A longing for something else
Which hopes abandons

Penetrate the fog
See to the center of things
The light of the wise

'What is the answer?'
Is not as important as
'What is the question?'

Start with epic fail
Search, quest, wonder, question, find
End with epic gain

Worry when you should
When not to means the world's end
So, when should we fret?

Stargaze now and then
Look up from the road ahead
As a reminder

Brach of public trust
Flaunt your mistake to the press
Loss of confidence

A small, thin error
Don't see it as a mistake
View the end success

Pounding waterfall
A thunder of life and sound
How does it calm me?

Accept your failings
Do your best to correct them
You'll accept other's

Many ways to see
Our global community
So small and fragile

Calm yourself right now
We act like naughty children
Sit down and be still

All the world's wisdom
If heeded by everyone
Could bullet-proof life

Don't hate misfortune
Do you want to stay a child?
We grow through ill-luck

A fool often says
"Because you can't disprove me,
You must believe me."

Don't fear the midnight
Of ignorance's horror-trek
Light is soon nearby

Wait for wonderful,
You'll find the wait wasteful
Love today's treasures

I long for love's balm
To dilute wisdom's coldness
Can they co-exist?

Act now, when you must
Action beats a soul's promise
To wait is to miss

A torrent of force
A hurricane of movement
Details in action

Thinking rules us all
Sometimes we need instinct too
To act without thought

Patience does blanket
All who view it in action
With a peaceful calm

Love is number one
The engine of life's progress
Wisdom is second

Let your mind run wild
Treasure your flights of fantasy
But, grasp the anchor

Don't school me too much
Can you heed your own advice?
Do you need it more?

Stand down and silent
Foolish advice giver, you
Mine is not to hear

Let me advise you
Even though I need it more
This is just ego

Sweet, loving concern
Always holding close to heart
Lessons of caring

'bye to yesterday
What did we know anyway?
Learn its lessons past

Don't cry for 'once was'
What 'once was' will be again
Treasure it this time

Love your possessions
They make a great soul's anchor
Feel them weigh you down

As the years tick past
Learn great lessons to pass along
Don't just get older

Who smiles in distress?
Those with wise maturity
Strive to be like them

When you are fatigued
Remember these two sure cures
Laugh and lots of sleep

What does make you laugh?
If it is something hurtful
It is not the cure

Laugh at someone else
Because they want you to laugh
This helps both of you

Move you smile muscles
It helps to remind us how
Use them or lose them

Beware false laughter
Laugh when you feel humor
Not just to make noise

Laugh just to make noise
You are robbed of the subtle
Joy real laughs can bring

The eyes can reflect
When a smile is real or not
More than the mouth does

Opinions are like
Armpits. All of us have them
And most of them stink

You must curb your views
You should know when to voice them
And when to be still

Do you believe it?
Or do you want to sound smart?
Silence is the best

Yours is a big world
How much of it do you know?
Always more to learn

Read all history
Know from whence we came till now
We are but a blink

See all around you
Hear with everything you have
These gifts go too fast

Take it for granted
But, remember to slow down
And appreciate

Full of energy
Movement is what we should be
But slow down to rest

Life's a hurricane
We live in a blast furnace
Learn to still your scream

Reign in your torrent
The eye of the hurricane
Make the eye your home

Search through the ruins
Find the answers to the 'why'
Human culture search

We are compassion
Empathy and sympathy
Holding others up

Look at your neighbor
Do you want to understand?
Look in the mirror

You care for others
Those in your circle, you love
Expand you circle

A helper for hurts
Cotton, stitches, bandages
Be a first aid kit

Love is not needed
If you want to help others,
Care is all you need

The pain of skinned knees
Stinging, burning and bleeding
The same for us all

"I love everyone"
These three words contain power
Show off your power

Compassion is all
You know a cut hurts, don't you?
It hurts everyone

Yell hate at a child
Like yelling in a canyon
Expect an echo

Like blades to the soul
Words can be blunt or knife-edged
Choose them with real care

You're inferior
To no-one, nothing, never
Inferior none

Our fear and anger
Come from the same place in us
Painful confusion

People like their fear
We feel so full and alive
Anger is the same

Can't think or reason
I lose my calm and patience
I must be angry

Where does patience go,
In a burst of fear-filled wrath?
Calm replaced by pain

Read more and speak less
More input and less output
Feeds your mind and soul

Don't say you are wise
This is to invite dissent
Be wise; be silent

DROWNING SOUL

By
William Armstrong

Poetry in 5-7-5 and
5-7-5-7-7 beats

Evil compulsions
These are what you must conquer
You could rule us all

What's impossible?
Does it mean we shouldn't try?
That's the possible
The search for what is distant
Your success is in trying

Showing self-control
Doesn't mean you lack feelings
They just don't rule you

Such a tough summer
Most of it spent in the rain
Waiting for sunshine
Termites chew the house apart
Carpenters rebuild it well

When you are depressed
Lift those who are also low
Find your spirits raised

The parade sprints past
The rain leaves me cold and wet
Shivering warms me
An armed forces float glides by
Led by horses and banners

When sadness grips you
Don't dwell on happier times
That is not the way

A green-gold leaf drops
As it falls, my sadness grows
Harvest of autumn
Does winter hold any warmth?
Touch lit matches to tinder

The more that we learn
The more we doubt what we see
We seek more answers

A teacher has taught
I can now love the lessons
Where is the profit?
Bush strokes of nature paintings
Do not pay my food and rent

Keep hope always close
Thunder will follow lightening
Clear skies after rain

A song of struggle
Beats and notes sound readily
A cool, calming breeze
As in my youth on the pier
I cry for long, long ago

Don't disdain evil
The few souls it has captured
Suffer for us all

I'm torn rice paper
Words written on me falter
Few whole fibers left
I try to be papyrus
Lessons learned at denial

Actions define us
The weak give up the small ones
The strong persevere

A jaguar roars
He doesn't prowl; he watches
Old and weak; past it
Sleep is his calming balm now
Watch him and be comforted

Prove you're a true friend
Mix support with honest truth
Both will be believed

Two hummingbirds fight
Each hungers for the honey
Their long beaks questing
A whirlwind of wings and claws
A firestorm of longing

Passion's prisoner
The truth cannot move from it
Like us in quicksand

Dirt and leaves and rot
Sun shines between the shutters
Window frames broken
There is no front porch
Some snow on the roof

Kindness, compassion
If you would have all love you
Make these your habits

My cat adores me
Purring when I stroke her back
Begging for my food
She sometimes complains of me
And whispers of her hunger

Maintain composure
Do not be a spectacle
Shallow gets nothing

A reddish-brown rose
Full nurtured by Spanish soil
Weeds choke her bud
Her heady scent makes me reel
She knows he's not good enough

Keep what you say real
Not all want your opinion
Truth shouldn't be harsh

A stork starves and dies
Is the stork a metaphor?
Dried-up cabbage patch
Predict tomorrow a fog
Cold, lonely Zen example

Keep you tongue in check
Speak truth as if all listen
And not all agree

A warm, cool autumn
It's all about thanksgiving
Stir the calming breeze
A yellow, dusky morning
Sharpened turkey knife

Live in the middle
Avoid the harshness of poor
And problems of rich

Leaving Halloween behind
Goodbye to the horror show
Fall falls gently now
Shocks are blunted by coolness
Pain, stilled by understanding

Your words in action
Teach with few words, act with more
Show others the way

Know the source of pain
Worms devour coffee beans
Fireflies point the way
Bees sting my camellia bush
And I know of true beauty

Be friends with the bad
You'll find yourself hanging high
Above the abyss

Green, yellow, orange
Sweet Autumn warm dry coolness
Some dust-spattered leaves
Rich, full, tasty vegetables
I am mirrored and mined for meals

It is difficult
Repay rudeness with kindness
Be above the norm

Warm, lasting Autumn
Breezes, cool drinks of water
Summer's blast evolves
Crippled life becomes normal
A hummingbird heals my pain

Practice only good
Our time on Earth is finite
Know you have triumphed

Cinnamon, nutmeg, turkey
Store-bought pilgrims, paper leaves
Sweet potato pie
My fear of a carving knife
Giving thanks for love's dinner

Make your promises
Don't keep them, you lose your way
Keep them, you find it

A wind shivers me
Wonderful summer's goodbye
Autumn settling
Warm coats and long-sleeved knit shirts
Fallen trees regrown

Do not just promise
They are empty, without form
Keep obligations

The sun is still warm
Noon feels like evening falling
Nighttime is soul-black
There is comfort in the dark
A light vacuum for my pain

Don't be like a swamp
Muddy, unfirm and unwanted
Be like solid ground

All over the world
Seasons catch my hungry eyes
Nature's colors call
So, I reach out to find them
And smile in my futile search

They live, who are good
After death, their good lives on
Death is for the bad

A life of growing
Growing in long protein strings
Growing through nurture
Growth comes easily to Earth
Death must follow life and growth

Expect misfortune
When things are how you want them
You will be prepared

A golden-brown haze
It dims the cool, blue, silver sky
Alive and clogging
Shortening a too-short life
Wasting a too-brief moment

In prosperity
Be prepared for some hardship
Will soften the blow

A chatter-roar noise
A Doppler sound, come, then gone
Riding the city
Collecting helmet critters
Singing the freedom found

Enjoy your money
It is there to enhance us
But, be careful, too

Cool, blue unity
A wave of least resistance
All are swell flying
Lots of sand and seashell loot
Hearing and sensing the end

Prudence is the way
Money is great blessing
Don't make it a curse

Let the professionals
Watch talent and mind prevail
Meddle not with it
Your knowledge is scanty now
Don't watch your pride let you down

Calm your want for cash
There's more to life than money
It is just a tool

Wet misted vision
North storm flowing, drenching us
Rooftop waterfalls
Humid scented thunder pounds
Lightening flash crackle lessons

Work for you success
Lead in all your endeavors
But, remain calm, too

The snap of wet twigs
Leaf weight rain-heavy branches
Weak leaves cry and drop
Autumn water ought to fall
Grow the wet pile on the ground

Brag, you're something new
Tell us, no-one has seen this
You are much deceived

After-rain scented
Fresh smelling wet dusty dirt
Up-splash from water-down
Crystal reflecting tear drops
Precipitating heart-burst

The wise grow one way
By learning to live through loss
This is how we grow

Orpheus in hell
Strumming a lyre of healing
Classic strength alive
Classic tears to show us how
Playing notes to show us why

A garden needs care
Water it with heart and soul
To see it blossom

Called fall, cold Autumn
An end to muted colors
Stilled breezes silenced
Gentle, warm, moving colors
Just ahead, white, mounded snow

Be full with content
Learn what other creatures know
Contentment means full

Gone leaving season
Leaving leaves steeped, steaming heat
Tall fall going, gone
Love's shove showing below us
Tickle wick blown out

Look fear in the face
And then, your life will move on
And strength will be yours

See our 'us' growing
Trust our dust to solid ground
Loving governing laid bare
See all of 'me' in us all
Keep our cheap 'cheep' in silence

We are truly one
There is never 'them' and 'us'
We are unity

Golden fall folding
Silver-white winter opens
Red, yellow, green spring
Our life in myriad tastes
Your life is one-of-a-kind

What is our true foe?
Since all life is together
We are the culprit

Patience is plodding
Do nothing by halves or haste
Your efforts will fail
The slow-cooked meal tastes richest
Stir the pot and let simmer

Such thing as freedom?
No, it doesn't exist here
Chained to what is real

Your frame of mind rules
Poor does not mean unhappy
Sick does not mean death
Love the life you have, not want
You should decide what you need

What is real freedom?
Is it freedom from work?
To pursue our dreams?

Do you fight often?
Do you find yourself angry?
Do you want to yell?
'cause you are dissatisfied
Not with others, but yourself

True freedom can come
Once we learn to cope with life
And its ups and downs

Do they laugh too much?
Do they find humor always?
Even in the sad?
There are two reasons for this
They hide anger or sadness

Pain need not chain us
Once we learn to blunt its edge
And to stand and move

Worry is a lie
Anxious is an illusion
Your stress is useless
Believe it when you see it
Then, take care of the issue

Freedom from our pain?
Always find a doctor's help
Never fight alone

Oil is made by time
Gold is made by molten heat
Diamonds, by pressure
Tough times make a person grow
Life's bumps see us much tougher

Feel what you have to
And use it to move forward
Otherwise, you crack

Chill-wrapped autumn end
Afternoon still warm-cool breeze
Let's hope for more rain
Fashion-layered clothes-horse time
People seeing holidays

Build on the tiny
Learning step by learning step
To find your summit

Wisdom and virtue
Do they set our happiness?
Money, just so far
For, if the money goes,
What else to make us happy?

Do not hate your past
Keep yourself grounded in 'now'
Your past put you here

You should yourself
You must think of number one
Life is just for you
Think of yourself before all
Then, open your heart to all

Do not make it worse
Do a little, if you can
Bit by bit heals all

When you find yourself
That is only half the search
It has just begun
Now the real work has started
To find yourself in others

Trust to your instinct
If you find that you cannot
Then, trust in others'

Does something hurt you?
Is there something that damages?
Does something cause fear?
Then, recognize the damage
Do not do that to others

Do not self-pity
It is wasted energy
And you remain weak

Wrong choices mold us
A person of bad choices
Can find strength to change
But, a truly bad person
Can not be made to raise up

Sorry for yourself?
Sometimes, it's appropriate
Don't let it linger

The way of envy
When the mighty have fallen
And been too outshined
To speak as inferior
Those who have surpassed their place

Things seem bad for you
Things seem bad for everyone
Widen your world view

Middle-road riding
Extreme pleasure can soon fade
Temper the extreme
It is our human nature
Extremes are blunted by time

Appreciation
Our gratitude in action
Helps lighten our load

Sure, you find roadblocks
Every great effort has them
They're a part of life
They are what we need to win
Or none are impressed

Procrastination
How long do you plan to wait
To make your life great?

Strive towards every goal
See the dream in front of you
Work at it always
Don't value the end too much
The end might not satisfy

Why wait 'til later?
Life is happening right now
Get yourself moving

Prepare for bad times
Even if they don't happen
You should be wary
So, even in your good times
Be cushioned for disaster

Climb each rung higher
Step by weary step you move
Will you reach the top?

Action is the means
Don't be content just to know
You must also do
Do not just learn of a thing
Make what you learn part of life

Give yourself a goal
Have something that you achieve
That is your success

Harsh words are just that
Sounds and air said by the weak
Their truth is shallow
And as you grow and strengthen
Those words will sting less and less

Give critics the slip
Avoid their prying eyeballs
Don't give them your life

Surround yourself well
Take care with whom you are friends
They are part of you
As well as what you read from
Learn from words of hope and love

Anger has reasons
Argue in favor of rage
You will always lose

Take care not to brag
Don't boast of hoped-for success
Be sure of your plans
Wait until you have it all
You will be admired, not scorned

There's no real reason
Scream if you have to holler
The echo will fade

Approaching winter
Freezing heart-fires chilled stilling
Fanning fires ice-calmed
Death-blizzard in harmless bits
Ice crunching afterward strides

Is your anger just?
It probably is selfish
Live by example

Snowflakes swirling lace
Tornado snow season puffs
Worry for safety
Stop to inhale the beauty
Newborn once-in-a-lifetime

Can you stand alone?
Can you state your point alone?
Can you last alone?

Fall song echo out
Dusky pumpkin orange fade
Cornfield harvested
Lift the blanket of warming
Stretch and light the fireplace match

Do what you cannot
Change what you think you cannot
Focus on yourself

Feeling comfort food
Nature's well-worn happy hearth
Handmade quilted bliss
Every food for every taste
The Earth holds us close to her

See the world as you
View all the world as yourself
The same kind of love

Autumn/winter fight
Fall warring with winter chill
Warming freezing ice
Ice cube chilling hot soup
An all-out, snow-laden douse

Admiration fades
The admired and admiring
Be disappointed

Who's insulting you?
Do you find the slanders true?
Then fix your problems
Amend your character flaws
Otherwise, pay it no mind

Laughter moves mountains
Humor can shift the burden
Smiles lift the dark clouds

Pleasure is easy
Pleasure is quickly found out
Pleasure can be bought
Satisfaction is the way
Strength, perseverance and love

Your intoxicant
Why not make it your new booze?
Get drunk on laughter

The ultimate choice
We may not have much freedom
But, we do have choice
Choice to be content or sad
We have freedom to choose these

You are your best friend
Treat your best friend with kindness
Love your best friend most

The sun now shines bright
The clouds split slowly apart
Rain turns to drizzle
I still can purr and meow
But fur hides my skin and bone

People do not fail
Possibilities can fail
People do not fail

If your life were filmed
Would anyone want to watch?
Is it an epic?
Life can be an adventure
Give you fans their money's worth

Once you get started
Make your success a habit
Keep the win going

Appreciated
That word is known to us all
We want to be thanked
But, do you return the 'thanks'
Show your appreciation

What we call madness
Is often a way to cope
With an insane world

Love's variation
Many are the forms of love
None of them show hurt
Violence is not the way
Causing tears is not the path

You are your best gift
And your best gift is just perfect
What gift is better?

The past can stop you
Look ahead to move you
Don't look behind you
Walking backward, you can fall
Walking forward, you progress

Gossamer heart strings
Strum them with a fine, light touch
A breeze can do it

Afraid of living?
Fear of success or failure?
Your fear is the pit
Make the attempt with your all
Give all of you and you will win

Get rid of happy
Happy leads to unhappy
Contentment is best

Live for the present
Be here now, to enjoy life
No past or future
Know that tomorrow will come
Tomorrow will be your 'now'

Keep your vision clear
Don't let suffering cloud it
See life past the pain

Enjoy 'eureka!'
Discovery is your way
Delight you've found 'it'
Nothing makes work so much fun
As finding what you've searched for

Don't make matters worse
Don't fight hatred with hatred
Accept and move on

Be more generous
Do not take without giving
This creates a void
Love will disappear for you
All that's left are excuses

Hatred can drain you
Do not waste your energy
Save it to grow with

The world is ready
You need to work for your dreams
This will take effort
Show you want to work for it
The world will be there for you

Hit the starting line
Ready yourself and then go
Cross the finish line

Review your mindset
If you choose to be happy,
Set your mind on it
You can be happy or not
You must make that choice yourself

Give the best of you
Don't demand it is returned
You'll see it come back

Picky is okay
We all have certain standards
Stick to your choices
There is no-one born perfect,
Only born perfect for you

Make a search for truth
Once you believe you've found it
You must keep searching

Look past the beauty
Of course, see the package first
It helps decide us
But, the real gift is inside
Does the outside match the in?

Things are rough for you
Life makes it tough to go on
Others have it worse

Actions are our 'me'
What we do is our function
They are who we are
Not our promises, our words
These in motion inform us

Do not wait to act
The moment has just passed by
Do not wait again

Look past the beauty
Of course, see the package first
It helps decide us
But, the real gift is inside
Does the outside match the in?

Things are rough for you
Life makes it tough to go on
Others have it worse

Actions are our 'me'
What we do is our function
They are who we are
Not our promises, our words
These in motion inform us

Do not wait to act
The moment has just passed by
Do not wait again

Communication
We live as social beings
We must speak of us
But, words don't replace actions
What we do is who we are

Know and set limits
Too much kills the appetite
Wanting means searching

Your friends are your self
Look at who you keep close by
They tell your story
We gravitate towards ourselves
We look for support from us

Kindness is the way
It blunts swords and stills anger
It's easy to give

Your birth does not tell
Who we call 'common' are not
Ask the 'common' why?
All are born of two parents
All need air to live

How do you see things?
As they are or seem to be
Fix your view of life

Why must the sun set?
Why must we need 'finish'?
Why can't it 'forever?
There are no ending, just change
It is nature's way, to change

Like all livings thing
Growth is the natural way
It's life in action

Earth's community
Global unity and love
Peace for humankind
We can be all of one mind
Love is possible for us

CRYING SOUL

Modern Haiku in 3-2-4 and
5-7-5 Beats

By
William Armstrong

Rhyming strong
Instead
Watch the stars pass

Moon over Athens
Lights my way along the path
Follow old footsteps

All is sex
Sell it
Television

In love with another
I am a bug on the move
"Forgive me, my love…"

Bring it home
Sing me
True and honest

Pall of depression
A warm blanket of lost hope
See it and you'll weep

Armchair leg
High heels
Pussy pillow

Firm and round and soft
"Don't squeeze them so hard!"
We're buying produce

Poor Yorick
The sap
Just an old skull

Deep space psychosis
Darkness belies the expanse
Breathe deep the starlight

Watery grave
Lifeboat
Swim for the shore

She nibbles my ear
I gently push her mouth off
"Give me back my corn!"

Yell my name
Echo
Answers itself

All around the world
People wait breathless and still
For life to begin

Bowling ball
Pins are
Nailed to the lane

Seeing all eating
Give a purpose to living
This is what life means

3-2-4 Beats

Heated breeze
Cross legs
Wishing for more

Stop the pound
Cry stop!
Wipe the tears dry

Cartoon fun
Sleep now
No night needed

Pungent rug
Broken
Vacuum sits still

Depressing
Assess
I pass the test

Words of hope
Today
Lost encounter

Cat is gone
Miss her
Back someday soon

Not bereft
Loving
You and I see

Sitting spread
Ready
Soft, strong, heated

Lying flat
Tension
Waiting sweaty

So, too, you
Little
Breaking my fast

Talons coy
Drop it
Yesterday gone

Full to burst
Stomach
Buddha near right

Funny man
Watch it!
Marbles punch line

Children sing
They should
We are old now

Serves you right
Assume
My love is gone

Tag a beat
Unknown
Call me writer

Meat/ cheese bliss
Not food
Climb that sky wall

Nature song
Always
Sing forever

Wisdom lost?
Never
Born with it, world

Cool, still, calm
Nature
Serene Action

Forever
Staying
Gone in no time

Aggressive
Wanting
Burst reaction

Sighing loud
Coasting
Life diary

Sing for me
Useless
Your angry soul

Days gone by
So long
Here now, present tense

Quid pro quo
Desire
Yours "No; mine "No"

I cause heat
Without
Even trying

Mother's age
My response
Is best said old

Ancient dance
Always
Falls short of wish

Freakish claws
Growling
Words of real hope

True courage
Catching
In spite of fear

The best day
Arms crossed
Love progressing

Stuck in bubble
Popping
Superheroes

Innocent
Sweet face
Nothing really

Brainy girl
Cheering
Sporting event

Metaphor
No rhymes
Don't understand

Pliant walls
Our mind
Only stops us

Perfect perk
Nipples
Bruised sideboob

Gold necklace
Stockings
Corset unbuttoned

Afterwards
Calm smile
Resting sated

Summer heat
Homeless
Layered clothing

Poet's block
Abyss
In remission

Sally forth
Persist
Nothing ending

Cute couple
Baby
Constant argue

T.v. face
Smiling
Living the dream?

Testify
Soulful
Cream of mushroom

Ages past
'member
Joust to the death

Stern Equus
Bucking
Falling from on high

Spears pointing
Dungeon
Such bad music

Mutton meal
Sheepish
Face turning red

Despairing
Captured
Parents are too

Harmony
Boy band
No bass, their voice

Fantasy
Girl group
What is the point?

Braided wig
Thirty
Don't need disguise

Serious
Facebook
Wants to have fun

Leads the pack
First wife
One of many

Protection
Sexy
Stripped of armor

Cross the lake
She's wet
What does it mean?

Butterfly
Don't move
Sits on blade edge

Tempered steel
Etched blade
Golden cord hilt

Scales and fangs
Breathes fire
Basho's dragon

Bad-ass girls
Fighters
Leather jackets

Runway strut
Spiked heels
Sword on her belt

Swaying curves
Slight bounce
Curly brown hair

Sight to see
Don't blink
So many skirts

Lotion spread
Tan legs
Don't want to leave

Legs are spread
Tan arms
I want to stay

Serious
Why not?
That's what life is

Call me sly
Cunning
Pick my nose clean

Calling all cars!
Makes sense
If cars are phones

Bratwurst dog
Baseball
Brown mustard cat

Mirrored shades
Her eyes
I see myself

I like food
So strange
Food likes me too

Do they hurt?
Tattoos
Now, don't you cry

Senseless
Just watch
Silly stupid

Snap my food
Send it
Looks delicious

Bottom lip
Stretch it
Over your head

Your elbow
Only
Into your ear

Calm the storm
Beach front
Twenty-foot waves

Strips and cheese
Before
Grilled hamburger

Triangle
Squared line
Circle no end

Prancing pants
See her
Mine start dancing

First chances
Starring
Insecurities

Pluck them slow
Heartstrings
Inspiration

Words of love
My soul
Penned in lyrics

Uplifting
Soul songs
Feed my soul fire

Sing my heart
Tuneful
Bass and treble

A good beat
Feel it
My heart's concert

Celebrate
Dancing
To my heart-drums

Can it work?
Will it?
Lyrical path

July heat
Matches
Songs of my heart

Sitting here
Writing
Red bump flea bites

Pancreas
Cancer
In remission

Battle scars
Torn up
Cancer weapons

Eating now
Wasn't
For a long time

Sell me stuff
Movie
Silent preview

It's all good
Music
New and old beats

Frontline look
Firestorm
World in terror

Pigs can't fly
Guess what?
Now they can talk

Blue pink red
Out there
Bring it back home

Numbered balls
Alone
Single bingo

Pyramids
Old, dry
Strong history

Rich in wealth
Go back
Ancient lessons

Ancient ways
Plural
Gods of nature

From the start
Way back
People don't change

Standing firm
Nerve meat
Tickle me right

Awesome flat
Perfect
So into me

Atmosphere
Simple
Dusk like dark dawn

Small portions
Bursting
Lots of money

I don't dine
Portions
I eat instead

Variety
Enjoy
Counter flavors

Opposites
Gourmet
Salty sweet fat

Recognize
Flavors
Synchronize tastes

Seasoned meat
Spicy
Tears to my eyes

Escargot
What? Huh?
Are you kidding?

Fast food fiend
Common
One of the crowd

Oh, I say!
Darling
Salad fork, left

All the rage
Trending
For five minutes

What the hell?!
Grilling
Antelope balls

Sour cream
Chocolate
Sinfully good

Spoken loud
Her point
She thinks I'm deaf

More money
Love it
Exciting fun

Strong as hell
Didn't know
I could endure

Life past it
Open
Much better now

Translucent
Pallid
Reduced hemo

So much pain
Worth it
Life afterwards

Food perfect
After
I.v. tube meals

Following
Cancer
Surgery dazed

Death's canvas
Many
Brushes with it

Pancreas
Cancer
Ridiculous

Remission
Beat it
My doctor knights

Very weak
No more
Severe blood loss

Years of pain
Gone by
Carcinoma

Life on hold
Rotting
Healed by doctors

Creeping cells
Eating
Cease and desist

So much time
So few
Hands for it all

Intermission

5-7-5 Beats

Vedic sages sing
Bodhidharma knew full well
Beatific smile

Trapped within my mind
Convince me to buy your food
Unsated hunger

In love with another
I am a bug on the move
"Forgive me, my love…"

Torn and soiled hat
A gift from a love of mine
Stolen from a corpse

A cat on the prowl
Caterwauling on a fence
Fur and claws videoed

Wrestling with fate
Put the blame where blame is due
Pollen on the wind

Await guillotine
My crime is one of good deeds
the sun burns my neck

Well-worn writing desk
Graffiti with a pen knife
Termites eat their fill

Face against a rock
Clouds of epidermal spring
The rock wears my smile

Running up some steps
Time is not against me now
Summer steals my sweat

Wearing a jester's hat
Halloween clothes everywhere
All the year round

Time to sell my soul
Yet another bad offer
July heat calms me

Sorry for the mess
Play your song for my parents
Your music sings spring

Captured by a knight
St. Invictus is my name
High dungeon windows

Gold butterfly dust
Silver firefly aether
Jade hummingbird wings

See me seeing you
A flash of jet-black cotton
I'm red with summer

Call me heart bereft
Desire your skin's surf and turf
Warmth for my winter

Why no children yet?
I am a big kid myself
Think too much just me

Why the long face, horse?
Are you tired of the saddle?
Your bridle too tight?

Fourth of July passed
Grills are cold and parties done
Independence gone

Don't understand it
What is this show selling me?
Strange television

July heat is intense
In the battle for comfort
July is winning

Summer remembered
Now I have electric breeze
Past summers killed me

Faces I don't know
What are they discussing now?
Life in all its ways

I only wonder
Are these words a new career?
Or just a hobby?

Sitting by myself
Me, myself and I
Just my life called hope

Sex, love, what's the diff?
It is easy to explain
Your care and concern

Pet gone forever
Another loving creature
Only a cat, right?

High up in a tree
Granddad throws down old pears
Storm waves crash

My lonely old pants
Pursue a different crevice
Stupid old trousers

Shrew bitch gold-digger
Why do I put up with it?
You in lingerie

Yellow-golden sand
Covers my feet every step
In an hour glass

Lonely droning bee
Wears a dress of white lily
Lining the asphalt

See me home safe, girl
I'll show you my gratitude, girl
You left too soon, girl

Always on top
Sweating under the covers
Bunk beds are fun

Muscles singing loud
A cry of "My god! Don't stop!"
Much needed rub-down

Breathing in her air
Our bodies smelling so strong
Car fan is broken

She grabs it, sighing
I feel the pain in my hips
"Give me back my wallet"

Stretched out, full to burst
Holding liquid I shoot in
A water balloon

Late night gaming gain
Green and greedy game gain get
Pc gaining game

Mirrored shades hide soul
Wide flow shoulders tapered waist
Bottom steel panties

Kick ass in high heels
Not a hair out of place, girl
Grab my sword for me

Simple times, my mind
Not for me, those complex thoughts
Thinking wears me out

Kick that leg higher
Show everything you've got
All that you can do

Must tweet everything
My life is fascinating
Not boring at all

July heat continues
Feeling drained of energy
Fleas are peppy, though

Gothic lipstick spikes
Talons made of estrogen
Curvy, creepy sex

Must be personal
Yet apply to everyone
It's confusing, right?

Pop goes the easel
Sing a song of time spent
Bling abounds with posing

Silly stupid fun
The lead doesn't always win
Fairness in action

Boarding the Metro
Rumbling above the train tracks
Forgot my ticket

Always on the lookout
Finding my muse everywhere
A patchwork of song

Too much forgiving?
Whom does it help, in the end?
A family died

What the hell is it?
A living, breathing fog bank
The thud of its pulse

You drink with wet lips
My rod is at an angle
As we try to fish

I call your number
My credit card is ready
I hate t.v. ads

Two pussies at home
They're tough and fun and are mine
Fur is everywhere

Nature's vast array
Paint the canvas of my soul
An apt simile

Legs to see and want
Soft and smooth and on the move
Walking on my hips

Breasts to make me drool
Moist and sweet and delicious
Fire roasted chicken

Curly tangled bush
A sweetly scented flower
Thorns prick my fingers

Your scent draws me near
A musk of thick and sweet air
Perfume counter girl

A tale of my city
So much movement near my home
Makes the world go round

So, I'm not a prude
I likes me the girls
More about my life

Spanish dancing girl
You flamenco through my mind
And leave me sated

Girl with a Mohawk
Beautiful, tough and naked
I dream I'm your choice

Heels and panties
Like a magnet for my cock
She wears nothing else

Always a lady
Coy and smiling at my heart
You see me melting

"My god. What a dick!"
"Never seen such a pussy!"
We're having a fight

Bobbing up and down
She glistens with drops of sweat
She loves her push-ups

"Not so hard, baby!"
"Which head should I stroke first, love?"
Playing the bongos

Passing the hours
I love the computer screen
A park down the street

Big, wide world outside
Early years spent wandering
Now I love four walls

A day of laundry
Adding soap and softener
To me or my clothes?

Love the overcast
Doesn't bring depression, no
Atmospheric air

Battled with cancer
My pancreas the enemy
Doctor knights triumphed

To battle stations
Incoming cancer bomb shells
I'm scarred from the fight

Claws, fangs, drooling hate
Bloody ripped and torn bodies
Beast from outer space

School girl sleepover
Painted nails and winsome smiles
Plotting mankind's downfall

Calling me to them
Twenty is all the rage
Buffalo hot wings

Round, sleek, crafted face
Hands moving smooth and precise
Brand new gold Swiss watch

Teaching kids lessons
Friendship, caring and humor
Some t.v. is great

Teach all tolerance
Show the next generation
Global unity

Living my small life
Going about my day-to-day
Ignoring the clouds

I bought a new watch
I'm proud of the way it looks
Isn't that funny?

Fear descends on all
Shadows over the city
Cries and dire echoes

Some want to see ghosts
Fear is excitement with dread
Life in the darkness

Disembodied voice
Crying for help from beyond
Imagination

Watching for spirits
Seeing what we want to see
Excitement and fun

Creepy foreboding
Walking slowly towards the sound
Wait and you will see

Calling to the dead
Sadness, loss and no return
We hope it's not us

Echoes in a hall
Footsteps coming, but no-one's there
Harmless, but is it?

Hyper-excitement
A voice on a recorder
Shocking, stunning fun

Don't you believe it
We hope to experience
Look to death when bored

Back into sunlight
Warm, gentle and full of hope
A cricket chirping

Perfect for growing
A huge expanse of nature
Ripples on a lake

As big as outdoors
Free of claustrophobia
Makes us want to run

Vacation from death
Drawn towards warmth and movement
Endings disappear

Pain is distracting
It pulls our focus towards it
Life is diminished

Quality of life
Movement inside and out
Thinking and feeling

Answer the phone
See who's on the other end
Is it your purpose?

Pleated skirt bouncing
Flashes of colored cotton
Moth to a bon fire

Again about girls
My gaze is so drawn thither
Seeing orgasm

Sports fun eludes me
Not macho enough, I guess
My bookstore loves me

Late dark-purple dusk
Shading closer to the night
Quiet window light

Stacks of green, coin piles
Easily gotten by some
Me, not so much

Turning a profit
Thick, fat stacks in my wallet
At least, that's the dream

Making snow angels
Arms and legs sweeping an arc
Gold\green money snow

Photo of my food
Steak, eggs, tacos, pasta, cake
Written on paper

Mild summer this year
No desiccating heat yet
A nice break from sweat

Honeysuckle arch
Huntington Beach house back yard
Home where I grew up